BY
Esme Hawes

SIENA

This is a Siena book
Siena is an imprint of Parragon Book Service Ltd

This edition first published by
Parragon Book Service Ltd in 1996

Parragon Book Service Ltd
Unit 13–17 Avonbridge Trading Estate
Atlantic Road, Avonmouth
Bristol BS11 9QD

Produced by Magpie Books Ltd, London

Copyright © Parragon Book Service Ltd 1996

Illustrations courtesy of: Bridgeman Art Library; Hulton
Deutsch Collection; Peter Newark's Pictures

ISBN 0 75251 571 3

A copy of the British Library Cataloguing in Publication
Data is available from the British Library.

Typeset by Whitelaw & Palmer Ltd, Glasgow

CHILDHOOD

As the twentieth century dawned, China, a proud nation which had once considered itself superior to all others, found that its infrastructure was crumbling and its economy was in ruins. The population grew continually but the industrial and administrative systems had been in place, largely unchanged, for centuries, and these outdated systems were simply unable to cope with modern demands. There wasn't enough food to go around; equipment of all kinds was in short supply, and urban industry was virtually non-existent. The Confucian ideal of large families had led to the country being cut

1

up into smaller and smaller farming units as property was divided for inheritance, while the sheer size of the nation meant that communication even between villages close to each other was very poor, and bureaucratic corruption was endemic.

While Chinese workers were constantly striking or disrupting production in other ways, foreign aid was effectively out of the question since China had always been an isolationist and essentially xenophobic country. By the end of the nineteenth century, the country was in a state of severe decay, and was governed by the Empress Dowager, Ci Xi, who saw no need for reform of any kind. In 1898, after her nephew, the Emperor Guangxu, a supporter of westernization, drew up a list of forty necessary developments, Ci Xi had him exiled and all of his friends were executed; she, however, continued to rule in his name. To the despairing citizens of China, there now seemed no way by which they would ever enter the twentieth century without resorting to violent action. Revolutionary groups sprang up throughout the land.

Hunan province was no exception to this pattern. An area of hills and fertile farmland in south central China, it was crossed and recrossed by travellers and tended, therefore, to be rather better informed than other regions. The local bureaucrats were relatively enlightened and, unusually, encouraged educational reform, opening the first girls' school in the country in the provincial capital, Changsha, in 1903.

The village of Shaoshan was located on the banks of the Xiang River in the very heart of the province and, here, on 26 December 1893, Mao Tse-tung was born in a hillside farmhouse, the eldest of three sons and a daughter. His father, Mao Rensheng, was a peasant who had joined the army to escape debt but who had returned to his native village and become relatively wealthy. He was a traditional and typical Confucian who demanded total loyalty from his children and who beat them frequently. Mao's mother was a devout and gentle Buddhist who generally supported her children in disputes with their father, though she disapproved of any demonstration of rebellion, declaring that this was anti-Chinese.

At the tender age of five, Mao started doing manual work on his father's farm. By the age of eight he was attending a local primary school, where he learnt to read, write and recite Confucian classics. At thirteen, in 1906, his father ordered him to leave school; he was to start working full-time in the fields, and enter into an arranged marriage with a girl four years older than himself.

Mao, however, had begun to read widely, and his favourite book was called *Words of Warning to an Affluent Age*, which pleaded for the modernization of China. Fired with enthusiasm, he called off his wedding, ran away from home and enrolled at the Dongshan Primary School in Xiangxiang, his mother's home town. Not long before he arrived there a severe famine had hit the area. The starving peasants had demonstrated against the government there, begging for food, and many had been ruthlessly decapitated. Entering the town, almost the first things that young Mao saw were the heads of the peasants mounted on poles outside government buildings. The sight, naturally, made a profound impression on the enthusiastic young man. A few weeks later, Mao's father arranged for a shipment of rice to be transported to Xiangxiang for sale, but the cart was seized by starving peasants, who ate all the rice. Though Mao thought that this was the wrong way to go about things, he lectured his father vigorously, telling him that he should simply have offered the rice to the hungry peasants for nothing.

STUDENT DAYS

At Dongshan, Mao came top in every class. He read voraciously, and collected a personal library which included works by Darwin and John Stuart Mill. He particularly admired George Washington, the hero of the American War of Independence of 1775–83. By 1911 Mao was ready to enrol in secondary school and he walked all the way to Changsha, the provincial capital, in order to do so. Soon after he arrived local radicals took over the city and sent letters to Dr Sun Yatsen, the leader of the Kuomintang (China's main revolutionary movement), demanding that he return from exile in Japan and save the Chinese people. Mao, too, wrote to Dr Sun and, caught up in radical fervour, cut off his pigtail (a sign of servitude which the Chinese were made to wear by the Manchus; abandoned when the Republic was established in 1912) and abandoned school in favour of a heroic revolutionary life. Enlisting as a private in the local army, he was disappointed to spend the next six months idly sitting around reading newspapers.

Mao drifted aimlessly for a while until he entered the Hunan Normal School in spring 1913, where he remained for the next five years in what was to be one of the most fruitful periods of his life. The school was a teacher-training college and the broad curriculum encompassed both traditional and contemporary thought. Mao was lucky enough to be taught by a man who had been educated in both Japan and England and it was he who introduced Mao to youth movements throughout the country and who encouraged the young enthusiast to write for a brand-new radical review, *New Youth*, which was then being printed in Beijing. Mao wrote an article about physical fitness for this journal, and saw his first words appear in print in 1917.

He developed a routine which he considered to be both revolutionary and disciplined. Rising early every morning, he would begin the day with a cold bath and then take a swim in the local river. He would then walk to college, whatever the weather, and, at weekends, would go mountain climbing in the nude, an activity he considered to be healthy. At the same time, Mao became the secretary of the local students' union and was heavily involved with the personal struggles of many of its members, even helping one student to get out of an arranged marriage. He also founded the 'Association for Student Self-Government', the aim of which was to wage war against unreasonable administrative demands. In April 1918, just a month before his graduation, he set up the 'New People's Study Society', and at its first discussion group declared that religion, capitalism, autocracy and Confucian morality were 'the four demons of the empire'. Eager young classmates listened on as he told them that they should now embrace the methods depicted in his favourite action novel, *All Men Are Brothers*, and that they should all take to the hills, become warriors, and fight for a better world. Mao's friends were impressed. The rest of his spare time, however, was taken up with writing romantic poetry.

Though the world outside was, to the Chinese, a confusing and remote place, all the students knew by this time that in 1917 there had been a revolution in Russia and that communism as a form of government was, therefore, a real possibility. The first Chinese Republic, led by

Mao Tse-tung

Sun Yatsen after the Chinese Revolution of 1911, had brought about the collapse of the Manchu dynasty and the abdication of the boy-emperor who had succeeded Ci Xi on her death in 1908. The Republic, however, soon collapsed in disarray and Sun's successor, Yuan Shikai, had died in 1916, leaving behind him a tremendous fight for power amongst the various local warlords, who were largely determined simply to carve up the country between them. Back in Changsha, Mao and his friends wondered why their fellow countrymen couldn't follow the model set by Russia and join together in a unified nation of equal citizens. Mao Tse-tung decided to go to Beijing and find out. In the capital he met the editor of *New Youth*, a university professor and one of the few people in China who really knew anything about Marxism. The professor gave Mao a menial filing job in the library, and he started work on a salary of eight dollars a month, at night sharing a bedroom with seven friends. He was utterly miserable, and was made more so because instead of receiving a revolutionary welcome, he was totally ignored in every debate he attended. Unable to bear the indignity, after just a few months he returned to Changsha, where he taught in a primary school and wrote revolutionary articles for the local magazines, where at least his name was recognized.

In 1920 Mao married Yang Kaihui, who had been a fellow student. Not long afterwards Lenin finally attained absolute power in Russia, having crushed all resistance, and declared his intention to sow Marxism wherever there was fertile soil. He sent an envoy to China and as a result, in July 1921, the first ever Chinese Communist Party Congress took place in Shanghai. Two delegates were sent from each of the six designated Communist regions in China; Mao was one of the pair sent from Hunan. The meeting took place in the utmost secrecy at a girls' boarding school. When the authorities got wind of the location, they raided the building, causing the delegates to flee in disarray. They eventually completed their discussions aboard a holiday cruise boat on a nearby lake.

Ambitious for control of China, the Soviet Union's leadership encouraged the Chinese Communist Party to form a splinter group within the nationalist Kuomintang, which was itself keenly supportive of the new regime in Russia. Mao co-operated energetically and was soon promoted to the Executive Central Committee (the Communists were by now in alliance wih the Kuomintang); from such positions, he believed, the Communists would eventually take over by means of subtle and patient infiltration.

Mao Tse-tung in 1925

COMMUNISM

By the mid-1920s Mao had realized that China's greatest resource was its huge, mainly rural, population, and that the way to success for communism was in the manipulation of this peasant power. Hunanese peasants were in a state of almost constant revolt, and Mao sought to harness these protests into organized mass movement, to the fury of the governor of Hunan. Mao escaped to Canton, and in 1927 wrote a report declaring that real power in China lay in rural areas. This indicated his first real split with Russian communist theory, for orthodox Marxism stated very clearly that power lay in urban areas. He also declared that 'armed struggle' was the only way to achieve real change.

The Kuomintang, meanwhile, remained the dominant political power, and continued to oppose the theory of radical land reform that Mao and the Communists espoused. Aware of the growing threat from the Communists, the Kuomintang decided to eradicate them. They began in Shanghai in April 1927 by murdering as many known communists as they could lay their hands on. Moscow encouraged the remaining communists to set up military factions in the countryside, and one of the keenest to follow this path of resistance was Mao Tse-tung. Then in 1928, under Chiang Kaishek (who had succeeded Sun Yatsen on the latter's death in 1925), the Kuomintang became the effective govenment in China.

Calling his men to arms, Mao managed to

mobilize four regiments of peasants, miners and Kuomintang deserters, and he named this scratch force the 1st Division of the First Peasants' and Workers' Army. He was convinced that hundreds of other peasants would simply take up arms and follow him, but when they did not his initiative proved a disaster. Two of his regiments began to fight each other, and two were wiped out by Kuomintang troops. There was little that Mao could now do save flee to a remote mountainous region between Hunan and Jiangxi with his surviving 1,000 soldiers.

Establishing his first permanent base, Mao was soon joined by a number of other notables, though his failure to rouse the peasants had now earned him an official rebuke from the Central Committee, which sacked him. To add insult to injury his old job was given to one of his former classmates and this rival now insisted on toeing the official Soviet Communist line. Mao sank into obscurity on his mountainside; by March 1930, so little had been heard of him for so long that the official Communist Party journal published his obituary.

WILDERNESS YEARS

Mao spent the time familiarizing himself with guerrilla warfare. His band of rebels learnt to scavenge for food and enlisted the help of local villagers. He wrote a great deal and spent the evenings reciting his aphorisms and poems to his followers. He would then make them memorize his 'three rules and six injunctions', which, among other things, warned his soldiers against stealing 'even a piece of thread from the people'. Mao devised hit-and-run tactics and led small raids on local towns, rigid military discipline being enforced during these forays. By 1929 his band of warriors had grown to a

At a conference in 1933

small army of 11,000 men and their first cave hideout had become too small. He led his troops down to a new base in southern Jiangxi, and soon received the news that similar such groups were forming all over the remoter parts of China. By 1933 Chinese Communist Party membership had risen to 300,000 people and the Kuomintang began to feel seriously threatened. At least 2 million peasants were murdered or starved as the Kuomintang army burned every possible source of food for the rebels. (Among those executed had been Mao's first wife, Yang Kaihui, in 1930, and Mao had married He Zizhen, with whom he had been living in the mountains since 1927.) There was nothing that Mao could do militarily to counteract such an onslaught and so he simply decided to regroup in a better position. Between October 1934 and October 1935, Mao Tse-tung gathered his forces around him and led them on a 6000-mile walk from Jianxi to the north-west of China. The 'Long March',

With veterans of the Long March, 1937

as it soon became known, quickly gained mythological status. During it, Mao learnt about survival of the fittest, as did his loyal officers; he also learnt, through a series of skirmishes, how it was possible for just a few men to emerge victorious over a far superior enemy. By the end of the heroic journey, Mao was the undisputed leader of the Chinese revolutionary movement. In January 1935, in the recently captured town of Zunyi, Mao Tse-tung took over as Chairman of the Chinese Communist Party.

ALL OUT WAR

Mao was by this time forty-three years old, a rather gaunt, chain-smoking figure with long hair, respected rather than loved by his peers. At his new base in Yanan he organized a self-sufficient system and taught all his soldiers to farm, sew and live abstemiously. He went constantly to address local peasants, encouraging them to join the Party by announcing that, after the revolution, all land would be redistributed fairly and the peasants would get most of it. He spent the rest of his days reading, and it was during this period that he wrote his famous *On Protracted War* (1938), in which he laid out his principles for successful guerrilla warfare, especially against the Japanese, who had invaded China in 1937. Teachers and students began to flock to Yanan, one of them a good-looking, if slightly dubious, movie starlet from Shanghai called Lan Ping, who was twenty years old. Mao's wife, He Zizhen, with whom he had five children, was a teacher, and had endured the privations of the Long March with her husband. Though not exactly beautiful, Lan Ping was still a far cry from the average veteran guerrilla and He Zizhen didn't stand a chance. Almost immediately, Mao sent his wife to the Soviet Union for 'medical treatment', and soon afterwards divorced her. Then, in 1939, he renamed his new girlfriend Jiang Qing (green river), and married her instead.

Mao's supporters now fell into two distinct groups – the intellectuals and the peasants. Though Mao respected the value of the intellectuals, he firmly encouraged them to 'identify with the masses' since he believed, in contrast to Soviet doctrine, that to be of the 'proletariat' was a state of being, rather than simply an economic fact. Without 'thought reform' of the intellectuals, therefore, the revolution would never take place.

Soon afterwards, in late 1941, the Communists were fortuitously assisted in their military ambitions when Japan, which had been fighting in China since 1937, entered the Second World War on the Axis side. The Chinese now had powerful allies in their fight against the Japanese invaders; they would also receive arms, equipment, supplies, and the benefits of Allied military advice. Because the external threat was more immediate than the civil one, the Chinese Nationalists invited the Communists to join with them in an unlikely coalition to get rid of the Japanese. The Japanese immediately assisted Mao's plans by declaring him Public Enemy Number One, thus raising his status to that of cult hero in the eyes of most Chinese. By the end of the war in 1945, the Communist army – the People's Liberation Army – which was highly motivated and well organized, consisted of 500,000 troops; in contrast, the Nationalists had suffered appalling casualties, at one stage losing 700,000 men in just a few months. Following Mao's doctrines, the Communists were also constantly indoctrinated with political dogma, and soldiers often pinned one of Mao's speeches to the backs of their caps so that the man behind could study politics while he marched. Fighting resumed between the PLA and the Nationalists, and by 1948 it was obvious that Mao's army would gain ultimate control in China. On 1 October 1949, the Chinese People's Republic was officially proclaimed with Mao as its Chairman. By 10 December, Chiang Kaishek and the remaining Nationalists still loyal to him had abandoned mainland China and established themselves on Formosa (now Taiwan).

The People's Republic proclaimed, 1949

GOVERNMENT

Choosing Beijing, the traditional 'northern capital', as their administrative centre, the Communists marched into the city triumphant, only to find that they had inherited a system which had been in decline for decades. Inflation was rampant, while transport systems and economic policies and controls were virtually non-existent. Years of often chaotic struggle in the wilderness, however, had imbued the Party with incredible discipline and self-organizational skills, and they immediately set to work, stabilizing the currency and repairing the railways. A modern and extensive

Tanks of the People's Liberation Army

public health system was set up, initiatives designed to weed out the prevalent corruption were introduced, and the first Five-Year Plan (to produce iron and steel) proved to be an incredible success.

But internal problems were rife. China was still a vast country, and many regions were now run by Communist army officers who were essentially independent warlords. China's decision in 1950 to join the Korean War on the side of North Korea against the South Koreans and their United Nations allies, was primarily a ploy by Chairman Mao to redeploy these commanders abroad. It was, however, a futile one, for on their return they were all relocated to exactly the same positions that they had left. The Chinese military leaders resented Mao for having sent them away to war, and many now set themselves up in open conflict to the Chairman's theories, turning to the Kremlin for assistance. Mao, however, stuck to his old notion of the army as a collection of guerrilla fighters, and the belief that all soldiers should be constantly available for agricultural and educational tasks. The military leadership thought this was demeaning. They also agreed with Moscow that nuclear arms were crucial in order to maintain the balance of power; Mao, however, considered that a nuclear holocaust would be positively beneficial, since, afterwards, 'imperialism will have been destroyed entirely and there will be only socialism in the world'.

But all these differences paled into comparison beside the essential problem – China's economy. Mao believed that only the transformation of the human spirit could bring about material progress, while other Party leaders held that only material progress could bring changes to the human spirit. 'Revolutionaries are made, not born,' argued Mao, and decided that the key to success lay in

27

bigger, better farms and not in the process of industrialization which other Party leaders (and the Kremlin) desired. With this split, Mao began to regard himself, rather than the Communist Party, as the ultimate source of wisdom.

When Mao was elected Chairman in 1949, a man called Zhou Enlai was named Premier (he was also Foreign Minister until 1958), and there were still twenty-five non-Communists in the Cabinet at the time. Though Mao himself remained flexible in his political outlook at this stage, he was appalled by the gulf between the peasants and the educated élite, and he grew scornful of the value of formal education (despite all that it had done for him). He never forgot his time as an anonymous library assistant in Beijing and, fuelled by this humiliating memory, he also came to believe that university professors, in particular, tended to be the most resistant to his brand of communism. He grew sceptical of their ability to undergo 'thought reform' with any real conviction, and began to display a personal vindictiveness towards a number of leading intellectuals and writers.

By 1955 clear divisions had developed between the Party and Mao, who constantly harangued his colleagues at Cabinet meetings about the 'valuable proletariat' as opposed to the 'useless bourgeoisie'. Despite the Party's resistance, the Chairman's collectivization policy won the day. By the end of 1956, roughly 100 million peasant families had been incorporated into the Agricultural Producers' Co-operatives, though their crops failed repeatedly and many peasants chose to destroy their tools rather than surrender them for use by the co-operative as a whole. Food hoarding became widespread as a result, and the reform was declared an utter failure. According to Party leaders, it was all Mao's fault. In September 1956, encouraged by

Khrushchev's denunciation of Stalin (who had died in 1953) that spring, Liu Shaoqi, one of Mao's most consistent rivals, launched a similar, humiliating attack against his leader. Mao was immediately deprived of his position as Chairman of the Central Secretariat, though this was dressed up as a claim that he wished to remain in the background for a while. His hatred of the official Communist Party, and of Russia, grew to immense proportions.

Mao started a counter-attack which he named the 'Hundred Flowers' campaign, so called because it aimed at 'letting a hundred flowers bloom' – in other words, allowing people to express differing ideas. In this campaign, having identified the schism between China's 'people' and China's 'enemies', he encouraged all of those 'people' to denounce their 'enemies'. In good faith, many intellectuals, among others, began to criticize lazy or inefficient or corrupt Party apparatchiks. Mao was delighted – his concept had worked. Less than three weeks after the start of his Hundred Flowers campaign he called it to a halt, and used all the public denunciations to purge his opponents from the Party. 'All words and actions that deviate from socialism are completely mistaken,' he said – and then had many of the denouncers arrested along with the denounced.

THE GREAT LEAP FORWARD

While Beijing declared that the 'Great Leap Forward', a series of radical innovations that began in 1958, had been started 'spontaneously by the mass of the peasants on the basis of great socialist consciousness,' it actually developed out of Mao's primary belief in the value of 'people power'. In 1957 he abolished birth control on the grounds that the population was China's greatest asset and, within less than a year, had organized the relocation of half a billion people and divided them into 24,000 'people's communes', with all their private

A good harvest, 1959

property confiscated and donated to the state. Everything from food to haircuts was to be provided by the new collectives, and peasants were shifted from the fields to factories and ordered to work around the clock in order to bring about the economic miracles China needed. The peasants slaved away to the point of exhaustion, but now there was no one left in the fields to gather in the harvest and, when crops – such as they were – failed again, peasants began to collapse from hunger at their work. Party officials, anxious not to appear to have failed in their tasks, got round the problem by inventing success rates, which in turn led central officials to demand higher, even more ridiculous targets. Suicide became commonplace among workers, and regular trials were held for 'criminals' who had 'failed economically'. Members of the public were encouraged to come to court and heckle the 'criminals'. Peasant life in China had become a case of each for himself.

A poster of Mao' prominent in a Shanghai canteen

Factories also instituted a series of 'criticisms', during which workers would gather together and then condemn each other for laziness or for having spoken ill of a Party leader. Mao himself started an offensive against the 'four pests' – flies, sparrows, mosquitoes and rats – and declared that China could eradicate all four in just three years as long as people pulled together. Families were issued with insect swatters and then required to appear each Sunday morning and exhibit their catches. Party members stood by and counted each fly as it was dropped into a large collection sack.

By the summer of 1958 the Great Leap Forward was in full swing. Beijing encouraged 'backyard furnace' schemes, exhorting millions of people to produce iron and steel in makeshift ovens in their homes. All other manufacturing was stopped, and even hand-drawn carts were given over to the transportation of bricks and coal. There were not enough peasants left on the land to maintain the fields and the rice harvest that year was virtually non-existent and, because the paddies had not been maintained, was followed by flooding. Not only did many people starve, but the metal they had produced proved to be mainly useless. And still the Communists refused to give up. Party members charged from house to house demanding iron ore and confiscating pots and pans, even tearing the locks off doors. All the economic momentum created by the Communists in their first eight years was wiped out in just one, and the Chinese people were soon plunged back into poverty. Famine killed 70,000 people and, despite official policy, black markets sprang up everywhere. Meanwhile, the Soviet Union withdrew its technical advisers.

Mao Tse-tung still refused to accept that his idea had been flawed, and claimed instead that the Party had merely failed to carry it out properly. Opposition to his policies among his colleagues hardened, however. In December 1958 the government called a halt to the 'Great Leap Forward' (although some of its programmes were to continue until 1961) and, in a softening of policy, permitted peasants to retain control of their own houses, fruit trees and tools. In 1959, it was also announced that Mao had resigned as Chairman of the Chinese People's Republic (though he remained Chairman of the Communist Party), and would now 'concentrate his energies on dealing with questions of direction and theoretical work'. In other words, he had been sacked, a decision Mao greeted with bitterness.

In July 1959 Marshal Peng Dehuai, the Defence Minister and Vice-Premier, and a veteran of the Long March, sent Mao a detailed 'Letter of Opinion'. Although Peng began by praising Mao, he went on to list the shortcoming of the 'Great Leap Forward', and blamed the Party Chairman for encouraging people to make up statistics in a 'fanatical' way. Initially stunned, Mao soon counter-attacked. After some days' silence, he had the letter published in Party circles, thus turning a private letter into a public criticism. A week later came the main attack during a conference, in which Mao made a detailed denunciation of Peng, declaring, among other charges, that he was planning to 'sabotage the proletariat'. If his policies were now outvoted, Mao said, he would go straight to the countryside where he would recruit a new peasant army and return to overthrow the government. Fully aware of Mao's immense personal prestige, most of the generals pledged their allegiance to him. In October Peng Dehuai was dismissed and sent to manage a small state farm in the middle of nowhere, from where he wrote to Mao that his sacking had been a 'great victory' for the Party and that he could not adequately express his acute gratitude for his re-education. It made no difference, for Peng now became a lifelong target for Mao. He died in 1974, having endured eight years of imprisonment and torture at the hands of the Red Guards. The comradeship of the Long March between Mao and his close associates had been broken.

CULTURAL REVOLUTION

Whatever the struggles within the Party hierarchy, by 1961 many villagers were starving; most senior Party members, though they had not backed Peng, secretly believed that the catastrophe had been entirely Mao's fault. In an unprecedented measure, 6 million tons of grain had to be bought in from capitalist nations and peasants were allowed to start cultivating their own gardens and to sell off their produce as long as they fulfilled their nominated grain outputs. Leaders like Deng Xiaoping, then Secretary-General of the Chinese Communist Party, declared that any means of stimulating production was now acceptable. In other moves, a number of eminent professors were rehabilitated, while official publications were occasionally used to attack Chairman Mao in a limited way. As Mao grew increasingly suspicious of Party members, his wife, Jiang Qing, began to emerge as his main political ally, since she was almost the only person near him whom he could trust. (Mao had married her in spite of the protests of his Communist colleagues, and after agreeing to their condition that she should take no part in politics for twenty years. Those twenty years were now up.) He was fully aware that all of his efforts were being blocked by the Party and, unsure of his next course of action, retreated to his country house for a while in order to take stock. During his self-imposed exile, China's economic affairs were taken over by Deng Xinoping and Liu Shaoqi, who had replaced Mao as Chairman of the Republic.

Flood control works in Tachai

In September 1965, Mao eventually returned to Beijing and reconvened the Politburo Standing Committee, technically China's governing body, three of whose seven members actively opposed Mao. This was the first meeting at which Mao mentioned his newly developed plan for a 'total cultural revolution'. Though this wording seemed, to Westerners, to mean 'an artistic upheaval', that was, in fact, a horribly inaccurate translation. What Mao actually demanded was 'a full-scale revolution to establish a working-class culture', and Chinese Party leaders realized immediately what the phrase would involve. Deng Xiaoping expressed his hostility to the idea and, with no one to trust, Mao sent his wife to Shanghai in order to enlist sympathizers. Once there, Jiang Qing held meetings explaining Mao's ideas and encouraging her followers to criticize her husband's opponents, who included a number of leading writers and artists.

Mao takes the salute, 1966

In February 1966, Jiang Qing released a statement to the effect that though 'the Great Proletarian Cultural Revolution' might take decades or even centuries, it was an absolute necessity, adding that the army would be the chief instrument of its implementation. Party leaders, beginning to sense where all this might lead, began to disassociate themselves from anyone who had ever expressed dissension and, by 11 March, Lin Biao, Peng Dehuai's successor as Defence Minister, had issued a letter stating that Mao's policy was the only 'unified, revolutionary and correct' one. This was a significant move, since it marked, for the first time, the point at which the People's Liberation Army conceded that Mao's individual views were henceforth to take precedence over those of the Communist Party.

On 28 March, Mao's main rival on the Central Committee, Peng Zhen, was, with other important Party leaders, removed, apparently for plotting against the new policies, an event which marked the beginning of the full-blown Cultural Revolution. Peng Zhen had originally been chosen to head the Cultural Revolution Committee, a euphemism for a group set up to purge writers and poets who had voiced dissent. Some time later, he and his wife were dragged into a Beijing stadium and forced to kneel in disgrace before the masses. Though they had clearly been tortured they were still just about alive, and thus were unfortunate enough to become the first prominent victims of Mao's idea that 'living negative examples' were more powerful than dead martyrs. (Peng survived twelve years in prison, eventually returning in 1978 to help found Deng Xiaoping's revolution. By then, Mao had been dead for two years.)

Mao appointed a whole new 'Cultural Revolution Directorate' which was made up of his personal supporters. The leader was Chen Boda, Mao's private secretary, and the deputies were his wife, Jiang Qing, and his former bodyguard. Mao soon 'persuaded' one of the most famous writers in China to write a 'confession' stating that everything he had written in the past was valueless and that now he would turn only to the Party for guidance. Assaults were launched against all who dissented from the new Party line, and Mao denounced Chinese educational establishments for being dominated by bourgeois intellectuals who should, he said, no longer be allowed to continue in their posts. Dissatisfied students were encouraged to agitate against the system, and this call to arms was taken as a free-for-all licence for them to rebel against their superiors.

Nie Yuanzi, a prominent student radical, was recruited by Jiang Qing to intensify insurrection on Beijing University campus. Nie put up a poster in the canteen denouncing the principal of the university, who had consistently emphasized the value of academic excellence over Communist Party dogma. The principal hauled Nie before a public meeting and demanded that she explain what she meant by such extraordinary behaviour; most of the students, frightened of expulsion, stayed quiet, appearing to support the authorities. Jiang Qing, however, was not going to give up that easily. She informed her husband of Nie Yuanzi's 'harassment', and Mao immediately ordered that the text of Nie's poster be broadcast to the nation and published in every newspaper in the land. The date was 1 June 1966, and students all over China went mad with excitement. Tales of horrible oppression by teachers appeared on university walls everywhere, while some students began breaking into the homes of unpopular lecturers and smashing their furniture. Other members of staff were forced to march through the streets wearing placards denouncing them as 'criminals'. The nation's students were filled with a new sense of excitement, terror and, above all, sudden liberation.

Chairman Mao was delighted – 'Rebellion is justified', he pronounced. The students felt they now had a licence for anarchy. The *People's Daily* reported that it was time to 'sweep away all freaks and monsters', categories which, it seemed, included all academics and figures of authority. Mass hysteria swept the country. In a typical incident, a student in Beijing was selected to denounce one of her favourite woman professors as 'rightist'. The student refused, and was herself then denounced for lack of devotion to the cause. The factions supporting the professor and the student both claimed to be the 'true' supporters of Chairman Mao, but in truth most students were totally bewildered and merely wanted to save their own necks. Utter chaos reigned.

RED GUARD

On 18 July 1966, Beijing's Tiananmen Square – which had been extensively remodelled, on Mao's orders, during the 1950s as an ideological monument to Chinese communism – was packed with more than a million Chinese youths. They were all dressed in khaki combat gear and wore crimson arm bands displaying the words 'Red Guard'. Many of them chanted slogans from a small, bright red, plastic-bound booklet called *Quotations from Chairman Mao* and, as dawn broke, Mao Tse-tung emerged on the gallery of the famous gate wearing a soldier's uniform and a military cap. His aim

Crowds wave *The Quotations of Chairman Mao*

was to unleash the youth against all of his rivals in the Communist Party. 'They have the arrogance of the bourgeoisie,' he told the crowds, who roared their approval. In the face of such overwhelming popular support there was little that Mao's opponents could do.

Mao called the first meeting of the Party's Central Committee since 1962. His supporters swiftly declared that loyalty to the Chairman was the only yardstick by which true Communists could be measured. The Red Guards were encouraged to run riot throughout the land, and they did so to shouts of one of Mao's favourite slogans: 'Destruction before construction'. A whole series of parades for the Red Guards was held in Beijing, and by November more than 11 million young people had been brought to the capital merely to gaze at their beloved Chairman. A huge statue of Mao, festooned with banners stating 'Long Live the Chinese People's Republic', decorated the main gate in Tiananmen Square. In an atmosphere of hysteria, young people, often crying with emotion, constantly chanted Mao's name, waving their red books and leaping into the air whenever their idol appeared.

As the Cultural Revolution took on a momentum of its own, youth groups splintered into smaller and smaller factions which frequently fought amongst themselves, while individuals continuously shifted between groups in a bid for personal power. Red Guards ran amok in every city. Because of the power struggle between factions, the names of streets and shops were constantly changing, so that other citizens became lost, thus adding to the chaos. Many groups declared that traffic lights had been 'revolutionized' and that, from now on, red was to mean 'go' while green would signify 'stop'. In 1967, by which time the violence had reached a peak, the streets of Beijing were strewn with corpses and trucks

Mao leads a 9-mile swim in the Yangtze

cruised the capital, collecting the dead. Meanwhile, in a display of Puritan prudishness, sexual affairs were discouraged as 'decadent and counter-revolutionary'. One couple, discovered in bed by the Red Guards, were then paraded naked through the streets. The woman went straight home and hanged herself. The Red Guards exhibited her body in front of her house for four days.

Meanwhile, under the slogan 'the great exchange of revolutionary experiences', many young Chinese people were given their first ever opportunity to leave home. Apart from the mandatory trips to Beijing, millions of youths were sent on long journeys around the country. For over three months, most of the nation's railway system was dedicated to this mission, while back in Beijing, Mao used the chaotic situation to rid himself of his main enemies and further the careers of his supporters. Liu Shaoqi and Deng Xiaoping

Maoist poster, Beijing, 1967

were both sent away to work in remote farms; Jiang Qing was promoted to 'cultural adviser'.

Mao was now instinctively using all of the tactics that he had learned throughout his guerrilla years in order to overthrow a Party administration which was, nominally, much more powerful than himself. By January 1967, he had realized that the general anarchy and the state of near-civil war had now created the prime moment for him to dismantle the official Communist Party altogether. In his New Year's Day proclamation Mao called for a general attack on the Party apparatus; anyone who called for moderation was to be labelled a 'class traitor'.

More chaos ensued. Children were encouraged to denounce their parents. Fighting broke out all over the country, ostensibly between Maoists and their rival Party followers, but actually between any rival factions. By this time the Red Guards had realized their potential and could be neither stopped nor slowed down. This situation was aggravated by the fact that, due to the almost total shutdown of the economy over the previous three years, the majority of school leavers had nothing to do except roam the streets and smash things up. Peasants were shunted into the cities in order to operate the factories but they, too, caught the spirit of the times and went on strike – though their grievances were, in essence, in direct opposition to Mao's aims, since they merely wanted higher pay and better living conditions. For the first time in China's history, dock workers also went on strike, and the few foreign firms which still invested in China now pulled out. Many people took to lives of petty crime, as being the only way to survive, and though a good number of Maoists now tried to halt the tidal wave of madness, the forces that they themselves had unleashed had become too strong to control. Zhou Enlai, who was still officially China's Premier, stressed the need to end the chaos, but the only force now able to do this was the army. On 23 January 1967, Mao instructed China's military commanders to come to his aid.

MILITARY TIMES

Despite himself, Mao ordered the army to take control, though he also told them to give active support to 'genuine radicals'. Many of the army marshals had been opposed to the Cultural Revolution from the very beginning but, even at this critical stage, they could not be seen to be openly opposing their great leader. Marshal Ahu De, for example, perhaps the most revered officer in the whole People's Liberation Army, voiced mild reservations about committing the whole of his armed forces to the Revolution. He was vigorously denounced, and censured for such absurd and feudalistic hobbies as raising orchids.

At the end of January Mao ordered the Red Guards to stop raiding private houses and to return to their homes. The army set about restoring order as far as it could, but former officials were frightened to return to their old jobs, while the young people who had seized power did not want to give it up. On 11 February troops took over the central police station in Beijing, and soon began to exert control. Though Party offices urged general clemency, since otherwise there would be no one left to run the country, army officers increasingly used military force to seize control from the Red Guards. Troops moved into factories and communes and began supervising industrial and agricultural production. By the end of February almost half a million soldiers were being used to run China's essential services; in many provinces they simply slaughtered any unruly Red Guards remaining on the streets.

By March the army had almost regained control. Whole days passed without a single demonstration and buses once again ran on time – they now even had room to carry ordinary civilians to work. Shops reopened and it seemed that the military had succeeded in restoring a sense of normality. They had done so only by returning to the status quo, however, except that now the army had control, rather than Chairman Mao. This worried Mao, but there was little he could do since he had authorized the takeover. He decided to concentrate his efforts on getting rid of one of his main rivals on the Central Committee – Liu Shaoqi, Mao's successor as Chairman of the People's Repulic, and his deputy as Chairman of the Party.

Mao believed that Liu Shaoqi's supporters would certainly denounce him rather than risk their own careers (and perhaps freedom); he therefore had his enemy brought before a committee. Liu, however, knew how to work the system almost as efficiently as Mao did, and demanded that a full meeting of the Central Committee be convened to hear his 'crimes'. He knew that his fellow ministers would agree to this, since the hearing would then become a part of official policy, which would mean that, if anyone wanted to denounce them in their turn, the formal convening of the Central Committee would make the process more difficult. Mao retaliated by simply appointing four more of his supporters to the Committee – though in the event he still only managed a majority of one. A barrage of hostile reports about Liu soon began to be broadcast on the radio, and his wife was hauled before a kangaroo court with Red Guards as both her judges and her jury. Jiang Qing, meanwhile, publicly denounced Liu at every opportunity, and made long speeches to student groups, reproaching the army for trying to curb the powers of the Red Guards.

This renewed plea to radicalism swept through the nation and Red Guard groups once again started vying for power. Army units fought back in self-defence. In a large number of places Red Guard factions actually launched assaults on military installations; when Red Guards tried to take over command in Henan in May, Mao dispatched a hit team to help them. But the PLA was determined not to lose control once more, and, openly defying Mao, they slaughtered the students. This victory encouraged other army units and, in a particularly violent incident, more than a thousand students were killed in Zhengzhou. Foreigners, too, were not invulnerable and, at one stage, a British consul's home was invaded and all the occupants spat upon, smeared with glue and forced to leave the building. For the first time in years, foreign tourists were advised to lock their hotel doors and to carry their valuables with them at all times. By 6 June, Mao, realizing that he had made a mistake, issued an order forbidding the Red Guards to conduct private trials, break into council offices or wreck state installations. The army was, once again, the victor.

On 23 July, the military moved into Wuhan with gunboats, planes and tanks. The dissidents immediately capitulated, surrendering their weapons. Word spread throughout the country. Jiang Qing still actively encouraged violence, however, while Mao issued confusing decrees. Once again, a million people gathered in Tiananmen Square to call for the striking down of Mao's adversaries. The *People's Daily* ran a headline stating 'Kill them! Kill them!' and, for several months more, violent fighting persisted almost everywhere.

Mao turned his attentions back to Liu Shaoqi, who was still nominally in power, though disgraced, and his wife. Liu had now written three confessions and a 'self-criticism', but he still provided an easy scapegoat for a great many of Mao's problems. Almost seventy years old, Liu was dragged before the masses in Tiananmen Square and forced to confess once more. Meanwhile, pitched battles were still being fought between the Red Guards and the army. The Central Committee, since it had no choice, declared that the PLA would now become the principal repository of power, and more than fifty army officers who had publicly supported the Cultural Revolution were immediately dismissed. By 5 September, for the first time, Mao authorized the Army to shoot at unruly 'mass organizations' – this order, in effect, marked the end of the Cultural Revolution. Jiang Qing began publicly to denounce armed struggle and, since most of Mao's enemies had been forcibly removed by this stage, it now remained to army officers to fill the vacuum.

By 1 October many of the senior marshals who

had been vilified during the Revolution were once again standing in prominent places at the National Day parades. Newspapers and radio broadcasts openly contradicted statements which they had made just months earlier. 'Counter-revolutionaries' were executed at mass rallies, without any explanation other than that they were counter-revolutionaries, and large numbers of former Red Guards, ironically, fled to the ultra-capitalist Hong Kong. In January 1968, Premier Zhou Enlai formally blamed the Red Guards for the economic collapse of China.

Suicide became commonplace among former Red Guards. In July, Mao himself repudiated the entire organization, stating that the Red Guards had failed to unite and had not transformed their inner selves. With tears in his eyes, he proclaimed, 'You have let me down, and, moreover, you have disappointed the workers, peasants and soldiers of China.' By the middle of summer 1968 Red Guards were being referred to as 'anarchists', and it had now become the army's turn to impose 'revolutionary discipline' on 'class enemies'.

AFTER THE REVOLUTION

On 6 August, the *People's Daily* reported that Chairman Mao had sent a basket of mangoes as a personal gift to the peasants who were currently promoting his doctrine among Qinghua University students. The recipients of the gift were, apparently, hysterical with jubilation and the mangoes remained on the table for several days until they began to rot, at which point they were pickled in formaldehyde. The incident signified the onset of Mao's new initiative – the 'Mao Tse-tung Thought Propaganda Teams'. Under the forceful direction of army units these teams were to enter educational establishments throughout the land and 'persuade' the students to comply with Mao's new initiative which was to be called '*Xiafang*', or 'Down to the countryside'. This initiative would turn into the most intensive migration scheme in human history, and during the winter of 1968–9, over 20 million people would be shifted from cities to rural areas.

The scheme was effective because so many different factions had an interest in its success. Moderates believed it would expel troublesome Red Guards from urban areas, while the militay thought it would split up hooligan gangs, as well as strengthening the army in outlying areas. Military strategists were particularly keen to send people to populate frontier regions like Inner Mongolia. On 22 December, Mao declared that city youths should be 're-educated' by peasants and urged all parents to send their children to the countryside. By the end of 1969 almost half a million 'young intellectuals' had moved from Shanghai to work on agricultural and forestry projects. In many areas schools and colleges had been closed down for over three years (having been used in the meantime as Red Guard barracks) and, though classes had resumed in some places, large numbers of young people had missed out on their entire education. Mao still refused to help matters, however, by continuing to insist that formal studies be mixed with physical labour and that all exams be eliminated as examples of repressive and elitist oppression.

Though most young people had spent the greater part of the preceding four years reciting Mao's proverbs, they were still not keen to volunteer for farm work. Those who refused to move to the countryside, however, were simply forced to go and then given new identity cards stamped with their rural addresses. They were then unable to return to the city legally and could no longer claim food rations at their former homes. Many professionals committed suicide rather than risk being assigned to punishing labour camps thousands of miles from their families, while the peasants who were chosen to receive the youngsters bitterly resented the élite few who broke their machinery and complained all the time. Large numbers of young people escaped back to the cities, where they had to live and work illegally, often supporting themselves through crime.

Late in October 1968, the first Central Committee Plenum for three years took place and Liu Shaoqi, by then ill with cancer, was formally expelled from the Communist Party (though this was illegal). He was placed under house arrest and refused treatment for cancer, while his wife was condemned to twelve years in solitary confinement. Liu was transferred to prison where, denied food and treatment, and subjected to endless humiliation, he died in November 1969. Other opponents were dealt with equally brutally and a whole new constitution was drawn up in which Mao's thinking, rather than that of the Communist Party hierarchy, declared to be the theoretical basis of China's future. Marshal Lin Biao, the Defence Minister and Mao's greatest supporter, was nominated as his deputy, and Jiang Qing, Chen Boda (Mao's former secretary) and Zhou Enlai were all voted onto the Central Committee. More significantly, the other three members were all army marshals.

These marshals soon ousted Chen Boda, whom they saw as Mao's chief assistant, and thus a threat to them. When new regional administrations were set up, twenty of the twenty-nine area leaders were military officers. Chen vanished, and not long afterwards was reported to have died. In 1971 Lin Biao and his wife died in a plane crash in Mongolia, apparently while trying to defect after having plotted to assassinate Mao. Whether this was really the case, or whether the army had simply eliminated another Mao follower, made little difference to the end result – Mao's prestige had been tarnished, and his two favourites had fallen from grace.

LATER YEARS

Chinese Communist Party officials still believed that communism would one day rule the world, but now thought that there were more effective ways to spread the message. They also believed that a *rapprochement* with the United States would help to balance the growing schism with the Soviet Union, who now declared that China had been violating its borders. As the Vietnam War dragged on and North Vietnam turned first to the Soviet Union and then to China for assistance against the South Vietnamese and their American allies, the triangular power structure became more complex.

President Nixon's visit, 1972

Throughout the Cultural Revolution, foreign policy had been paralysed, and all of China's forty-six foreign ambassadors had been called home for re-education. The Foreign Ministry had been occupied by Red Guards and most of its records and other paperwork destroyed, but by 1969, when some 200,000 Soviet troops were aggressively installed along the Chinese border, a resumption of friendly relations with the United States became inevitable. China declared that it would begin talks with the arch-capitalists in February 1969; the Soviet Union expressed its disgust that a communist country could deign to collude with the imperialists.

The situation was explosive. On 2 March 1969, 300 Chinese soldiers invaded an uninhabited island in Manchuria and began shouting Maoist slogans. As Russian soldiers emerged from their frozen barracks, the Chinese troops started shooting, killing at least thirty men. The inci-

Memorial parade, Beijing, September 1976

dent triggered a host of skirmishes, some quite serious, all along the Soviet/Chinese border. This conflict, naturally, meant that China became increasingly pragmatic about its relations with the United States.

In April 1971, in an astonishing move, Mao invited a group of fifteen American table tennis players to tour China. Then, in February 1972, US President Richard Nixon and his wife visited Beijing, where they were treated in lavish style. This visit summed up the incredible turnaround in the country's foreign policy, for it was still just a few years since Mao had described Nixon as an 'ugly, imperialist chieftain' and had encouraged the Red Guards to storm foreign embassies and to assault the diplomats. President Nixon and Chairman Mao discussed economic investment and trade relations, and soon afterwards, in October, the Chinese People's Republic gained the right to a seat at the United Nations when the Republic

Mao Tse–tung

of Taiwan, which had claimed to be the legitimate government of China since Chiang Kaishek and the Nationalists had taken refuge there in 1949, was expelled by a resolution of the other UN members. Leonid Brezhnev, the Soviet leader, declared that any friend of the United States was the sworn enemy of the Russian people, but by 1975, as the Vietnam War ended and Japan assumed an increasingly important place in world economic affairs, Asia was, in any event, changing, both politically and economically, almost beyond recognition.

Before ever setting eyes on this new world order, Mao Tse-tung died in Beijing on 9 September 1976, aged eighty-two. Ten days of formal mourning were declared; once more a million people attended a rally in Tiananmen Square. Though towards the end of his life he had constantly reiterated the need for national stability, Mao was worried that a Soviet-style Communist Party would take over after his death, and had thus laboured to prevent the Party becoming all-powerful. During the Cultural Revolution Jiang Qing, his widow, and three of her close associates, Wang Hongwen, Yao Wenyuan and Zhang Chungiao, had formed a radical group within the Chinese Politburo (a team which later became known as the Gang of Four). After Mao's death, Jiang and her three colleagues tried to take over the reins of power as soon as seemed acceptable; in a desperate bid for government, they forged documents stating that Jiang had been appointed as her husband's successor. The deception was discovered almost immediately and the Gang of Four were seized and arrested, then subjected to a long trial. As Jiang Qing was handcuffed and led away she called out 'I was Chairman Mao's dog. Whoever he told me to bite, I bit,' but it was too late. All four members of the Gang were sentenced to long prison terms, and officially blamed for almost everything that had gone wrong in China during the past twenty years. (Jiang Qing allegedly committed suicide in prison in 1991, aged seventy-seven.) The Mao era was officially over and, though his presence remained to haunt China, and is likely to do so for many decades, it was left to his few political survivors to deal with the devastating legacy of the chaos that he had created.